CROW MILK

Poems by **Rick Agran**

March 1, 2003

To Jane on a
Deering eve —

Rick Agran

OYSTER RIVER PRESS

ISBN 1-882291-55-7

Acknowledgments

The author expresses his gratitude to the editors of the following publications in which these poems or poems very nearly resembling them first appeared. *Aegis*: "The Nature of Kisses," "Responsibility," "Shoes of One's Own Choosing," "Boys in Blue"; *dew*: "Compliment"; *Kettle of Fish*: "A Short Happy History of Our Life Together," "My angel"; *Fledgling*: "Deer Hunter, shot and left"; *Kinesis*: "Crow Milk," "It Turned on a Dime Like a Rideable Compass"; *Lowell Review*: "Cartwheels," "Shivaree"; *Portsmouth Annual*: "To Nancy (who taught me Catch 'em & Kiss 'em)"; *Portsmouth Review*: "At the Edges of Everything, the Children."

OYSTER RIVER PRESS
20 Riverview Road, Durham, N.H. 03824
(603) 868-5006

Contents

A place where marigolds fly from the tips of our fingers,
golden-orange sparkles of light.

Where silver-blue waves crest and roll from shore to shore
in our bathtubs.

Each face we see gentles in our presence.
Red maple leaves, the purest of love notes, slide under our doors.

A place where stumbling at the end of a sentence . . .
is holy.

a place where everything is cured by kissing it hello.

Shoes of One's Own

Shoes of One's Own Choosing

I met a woman with one blue eye and one green eye.
I knew her life like my own. I have different sized feet.
One small foot and one smaller foot leave me rocking
back and forth like a boy with a big decision.

The shoes that fit, I wear forever, the ones that don't
I hobble around in, never know which foot will do the sacrificing
until it's doing it. Sometimes I can hide it, the way I skip or glide,
but if you know me, you can tell my dance from my limp.

Black Umbrellas

On a rainy day in Seattle stumble into any coffee shop
and look wounded by the rain.

Say *Last time I was in I left my black umbrella here.*
A waitress in a blue beret will pull a black umbrella

from behind the counter and surrender it to you
like a sword at your knighting.

Unlike New Englanders, she'll never ask you
to describe it, never ask what day you came in,

she's intimate with rain and its appointments.
Look positively reunited with this black umbrella

and proceed to Belltown and Pike Place.
Sip cappuccino at the Cowgirl Luncheonette on First Ave.

Visit Buster selling tin salmon silhouettes
undulant in the wind, nosing ever into the oncoming,

meandering watery worlds, like you and the black umbrella,
the one you will lose on purpose at the day's end

so you can go the way you came
into the world, wet looking.

Wearing Dad's White Shirt Backwards

That substitute teacher in art, you could tell she was strange.
Black hair pulled back so tight her eyes slanted,
her ponytail bobbed as she walked the halls.

Her teeth brilliant and pointy, she chewed gum
that cracked in the corners of her red mouth.
She made everyone else spit theirs out.

Sitting crisp in a chair, she crossed her legs
at the knee wearing red rubber flip flops,
a red color we'd never seen before.

Today, class, we'll paint the foot, she said.
Extending her long, pale leg,
her ruby big toenail pointed straight toward us.

Billy dipped his brush in lumpy blue tempera
and ran it along the clean arch of her right foot.
Her head dropped to one side,

and she sighed at the paint's coolness.

To Nancy, who taught me

The day she slowed down, her red hair
streamed behind her as she ran, tickling my face.
Nancy was the fastest, most beautiful girl.
I only chased her once before, without catching her.
Weaving through jump-ropers and kick-ball players
we ran off the macadam into the grass.
Spring's hot buzz made my breath come harder,
a trickle ran down the side of my face.

Arm outstretched, my fingers barely touched
her red hair
and then she was in my arms, offering me her cheek,
hot and flushed pink with a rouge of exuberance.
I tasted the salt on my lips.
She bent to pull up her knee sock
and with bells ringing, we walked side by side
to our classroom door.
I let her go before me in line
just so I could look at her hair one more time.

In Loco Parentis

She was a conduit for gallons of water
I administered with ritual care
one ounce at a time, sprinkling the pink
plastic bottle on the back of my hand
to test the temperature.
Its nippled ball fit perfectly
into the socket of her mouth.
A small mouth, not large enough to smile
or cry, but able to hold a bottle
like a dog holds a tennis ball.
I never made the connection
that the bottles I fed her filled her.
She was demure, always closing her eyes
the second she lay down, not so much
as a peep out of her when horizontal.
She settled in, a good girl,
the water slowly trickling out
of the little round hole
between her chubby plastic legs.

Cakes Continue To Rise

A pancake with its burnt side down
is still burnt.
No amount of syrup can hide it.

And the heel of stale white bread
is not camouflaged
inside the peanut butter and jelly sandwich.

I've jumped in front of the oven.
Cakes never fall
as you have always threatened.

And baloney is not enhanced by frying it.

Spoonfeed me a rich tapioca
of truth.
I swear, I can take it.

Help me cut my uncertainties
into littler pieces.
You've always been afraid I'd choke.

Give me the lollipop of life
and I promise
I will run with it in my mouth.

Picked by Accident

1. Like Father

My baby-sitter was full of black coffee
and Pall Malls in the mornings,
full of bloody red wine and its boozy charm
when my dad retrieved me after his work.

Sharp at cards, crosswords, and cooking
she negotiated a life between the margins
of percolator and cocktail shaker
and their evenly spaced rotation on the kitchen counter.

Her husband's Black Label was the first beer
I ever tasted and the smoke from her Pall Malls
the first I ever inhaled. I felt awed by her,
a mixture of honored and uneasy

at the way her bosom brushed the top of my head
when I hugged her good-bye at the end of the day,
her belly soft and quiet at my ear.
My father was fascinated with her too.

After work they drank and flirted
across the kitchen table, faces flushed
with a rouge of alcohol and awkwardness.
Sometimes they stumbled up the back stairs

to speak of grownup matters. I paused in my playing,
stood by the closed door, breath held, supposing
they discussed in whispers my daily trespasses,
made detailed notations of my shortcomings:

wet towel on the floor, won't come when called,
unwilling to share, mean to her children.

Upon their reemergence my father's explosion
never came, just the easy sliding back down
to the kitchen, sighs of relief, cracked ice
in stainless steel, more banter and fresh cigarettes,
a breeze through the window to blow it all away.

2. Like Son

Bare feet quiet in the warm grass, I came
around the corner of the house to look for her
in the garden but found her above me
at her bedroom window.

She was climbing onto the roof to sunbathe naked,
the bounce of her breast cushioned in one arm
as she jumped down to the hot tar and spread
her towel like a picnic blanket.

As she rubbed coconut lotion on herself
I imagined I heard the veiled sounds
I had taken for their whispers, understood them
now as the sounds of surrender, a surrender new

and incomplete in my mind, standing below her
with one hand, palm open and out, the other
clutching a pink clover picked by accident
and fished from between my toes.

Drowsily she cooked dinner that evening,
tipsy and tan, while I floated through her room,
to her pile of clothes under the eaves.
I found her coconut scented brassiere,
investigated its round shape and sweet smell.

Confessional Basketball

I dream Charles Simic teaches poetry on the sidewalk,
the dirty seaside sidewalk in Seattle one day.
In a blue rainy fog, in a tattered blue bathrobe,
underneath it his white nightshirt apparent
like a slip forever showing.

We sit on the corner of Second and Bell while he paces
the sidewalk, talking and gesticulating—Wildly so.
He pauses to wipe the Puget Sound mist
from his round black glasses and then he stands still.
Still as a widower's teapot, uneventful
as a glacier's vacation.

He shows us a game of one on none, basketball in pajamas.
He makes twenty jumpshots in a row.
The net is made from the chain of old anchors,
silver-blue Pepsi cans from the 1960s
and shiny nickels stolen from little brothers by crows.
An indestructible net, its customary swoosh
is replaced with cold galvanized sounds.

His triumph is marked by a brief downpour,
which flows down Second toward the Sound.

I rest my black umbrella by the parking meter.

At the edges of everything ...

Crow Milk

You might say crows watched over me,
taking turns walking the rails of my crib,
singing, heads bobbing,
black throats rippling.

At sunrise they carried me wild purple grapes,
we shared black raspberries on the thorn
in the evening, a mesh of sugar in our voices
weaving us loosely into a family.

Origami

Halves

in the fall
as a kid
I folded

Then thirds

my blanket
as it got
colder
I got no
smaller

Then quarters

Iowa lullaby for a child in the field

Little one, wipe your tears, I promise
you will take off your clothes with quails.
You know their eyes
see sorrow's a grassblade high.
They know butterflies are food.
They'll weave you into a nest of sweetgrass.
You'll fly across roads rather than walking them.
They'll rock you to sleep as the wheat waves.

Responsibility

Eve was unimaginably blonde,
robust and glorious
brought forth from Adam in spiritual surgery.
Asleep in an orgy of deluded grandeur,
he didn't notice a thing.

Initially, a vague sense of loss.
Unnamed, he numbed it,
went off naming creatures,
although soon his longing grew
to immaculate proportions.

Adam couldn't believe
the Eve he'd borne was part of him,
her jaunt and insolence so beautiful.
Wanted to throw her down and take her,
retreating to forests of unharvested fruit.

She spirited him off into tall grass
and made love to him.
Welcomed him back
inside himself
and his rage was gone.

At the Edges of Everything, the Children

unloved, unbaptized, unwanted, unfed,
   the mortal infants of infant mortality, have returned
   to this earth embodied as crows.

In limbo, these children learned what to live:
   a petty thievery of the promised land.
      Steal quietly, little children, the shadows

of crows, black comfort, smallest of vehicles,
   beak and wing, raucous voice.
      Return to hop around the churchyard lawn,

to further inhabit an indifferent world,
   the unchosen wandering the sides of the road,
      the shouted at and shot at, solitary in sin.

Left to the fields on the edges of everything,
   but always there, crying,
      eyes ever upward and wary,

small survivors, newly made in shadow.

Shot and Left

Sound plays with the roof of my mouth
and fills my ears like bowls,
acorn top or two pinkies as if whistles themselves.
Silence between sounds, unsafe, hollow.
Ocarina of palm and hand, a loon-call trill,
this sound not possibly animal.
Not dark enough for fire,
utterly human invention.
In woods filled with hunters,
orange failed me, singing failed me,
buckshot failed me, and only the whistle song
with breath to make a presence out of nothing.

Assateague and Other Bedtime Stories

Assateague

Assateague is where the ponies swim to
driven from the shore to greener pastures
and there we set Bill to sea.
We carted the boxes around the night before,
to dinner, to the beach, sat him on the dresser
and blew smoke rings at him,
sitting there in an ashen pile, newly happy,
converted by fire to dust and smoke,
a loving man carried around
by his six year old niece, Brooke,
like a teddy or a dolly.
When she took out the boxes of his ashes
she said *This is my Uncle Bill.*
The labels read simply
"William F. C———, Partial Remains."
He was broken into portions, going home in pieces,
measured out like a tonic that soothes,
like yards of silk, like the life of a rose.
Half to Assateague, half
to the Calfkill River in Tennessee.
Brooke set him on the table
at the Legion Hall and faced the label toward herself.
Uncle Bill is looking only at me
she said, gathering the black plastic box
in her arms and resting her head on it,
the way someone might come up behind you
and throw their arms around your neck
and maybe nuzzle your ear and rest their chin
on top of your head and love you.
There's no place left for Bill but Assateague,

the serenity of surf and sand, a heaven of our own.
His lover in the Calfkill River six weeks ago
will flow out to meet him, will sing hello
in a southern-boy drawl sweet with pecan pie.
Tide's flowing past us out to sea, as we leave
the Legion and make for the waves, lights on
for a mile or two, parked in the sand
where the boardwalk ends, the ferris wheel
in the distance unturning.
The jetty is rocky but navigable holding hands
with friends to the end. Brooke grabs my hand
as we make for the rocks, she anchors me
while she thinks I anchor her
and we hop from rock to rock.
You're a little mountain goat
I say and she repeats it as an affirmation,
I am a little mountain goat and we hop the hops
that seem best and smoothest until the surf
splashes us just enough and she says
It is like a giant washer where the spray gets on you.
The salt whips in our eyes and ears
and the family and friends gather around with red
carnations and roses, read Tennessee Williams,
and the partial remains of William F. C———
are opened and blowing around
and everyone takes handfuls
and blows them, throws them,
lets go of them in the wind
and the sun sparkles on the water,
the waves crash on three sides of us

and Bill is spilled on occasional shoes,
patted on one another's backs and enfolded
around us as we hug and the flowers go next,
form a line in the sea as waves sweep out
and cue them up, a line of flowers
blood red flows for a quarter mile
and out of sight and Brooke says
The ocean is mad and crying
'cause Uncle Bill is dead.
Brooke handed him out like mudpie or candies,
sifting him through her small brown hands
and we all have a gray hand and a clean hand
and ashes on our faces stuck in tears,
drawing lines where they were
and this procession is over.
Brooke grabs my ashen hand with hers
and she says *Uncle Bill is all over now.*
and she tells me she wants to ride home with me
and she tells me in the car about the short cut
she takes through the neighbor's backyard,
that will be our secret,
that she takes it.

Cathedral, Washington DC 1993

Said the reverend, *You must face forward,*
look at me, don't look at your partners just yet.
We gather today in the company of friends
and lovers to make our commitments
to one another known. I ask you to take
your partner aside, take one another's hand,
look each other in the eye and tell him all the wonder
you feel at being here with her, tell her
the reasons you love him and let this spirit
work through the two of you, make this a moment
to reverberate through the rest of your lives.

A hush runs through the crowd, love's weepiness,
murmurs of vow and promise,
the strength of two joined and recognized as one.
One thousand eight hundred couples,
a gathering of friends and lovers join hands
to commemorate love,
to solidify that which is already solid
as men love men and women love women,
happy in this moment they are both touched
and untouchable in the power of a love
that transcends all, a love that says you may kiss
the bride no matter who he or she may be.

And then to step out into the world again.
I do.

One Circle

He still has his morning rituals:
coffee, toast and jam, a Marlboro
lit with a kitchen match.
Jack's lonely making himself breakfast
in the mornings without Peter.
Jack used to grind the coffee,
strong black French roast,
while Peter cooked Eggs
Sardou or Benedict.

Jack went to the beach last night,
walked the mile of quiet waves
that Peter and he used to stroll
on summer nights too hot to sleep.
This morning there's frost,
a morning that brings red and gold
to the swamp maples.
Jack's toes are cold in the kitchen
and he thinks how he used to be

the warm one. In every couple,
the warmer and the warmed.
He grinds the coffee,
this smell always new,
a minor rejuvenation.
He dresses while the coffee brews.
Puts warm socks on, flannel-lined jeans

from their trip to Maine. He pours
two cups of coffee, one for himself

and one for Peter. The trip down the hill
in the car swirls by in watercolors
through the frosted windshield.
One cup warms his right hand,
the other melts a circle on the windshield
where its heat rises. Passing through
the iron gate he drives to the back right,
to the black stone with the star of David.
He had wanted for Peter, a small statue

of Mercury, a handsome young man
with wingèd feet, because Peter never ever
stood still. Jack dips three fingers
in Peter's coffee, sprinkles it on the stone,
the steam from this christening rising.
Pours the rest on him, in the frost-silvered grass,
imagining where Peter's feet might be.
He drives back home thinking about breakfast,
empty cup on the seat beside him.

Newly Lost, Newly Found

Each poster is like a clear glass splinter
in the fingertip, disguised by blood,
it's unable to be removed. Like
Missing:
Sarah Ann Wood,
the lost child I wish remained lost
for reasons I'll explain . . .

Or **Missing: Tammy Belanger**
whose xeroxed likenesses got blurrier
and blurrier the five years we hoped her picture
would make a difference, somewhere, anywhere.
With age, the spark gone out of the eyes,
the gaps in her teeth getting wider
and blacker, almost a caricature of herself.

Surrounded by new images of Sarah Ann, at breakfast,
in the grocery, laundromat, post office, at the toll booth,
I conduct the everyday going on with my life.
Learning a month later she's gone completely, taken
to the woods, buried in red-tinged muddy snow,
the newly lost, newly found.

Eight years later I see **Missing: Tammy**
curled and yellowed on the side of a forgotten
cigarette machine in a one mechanic garage
and I, through force of hope, can picture her

twenty or so, disappeared for a reason
no one knows . . .

Happy in California, braids and bangs
grown out, freckles just as beautiful. . . .

Tethered

I miss you so much
I ought to forget about you completely
and act as if you never were. . . .

    *   *

You were the new girl in fourth grade
the face every kid turned to like a sunflower
as you clomped into the common room
in red wellies in mud season.
You rode a donkey to the bus stop
that trotted home when you hopped off.

    *   *

Little red ball and a handful of thorns,
you taught me the math and measure
of playing jacks, the rhythmic
toss bounce sweep catch.
One chance to grab what you could,
your small hand a precise blur.

    *   *

The boys said not to teach you marbles.
The girls would not let me play horses.
The year before, I was the new boy
collecting milk money class to class
so everyone would know me,

the job I passed on to you.
You ordered us coffeemilk on the sly.

*   *

I taught you to sweep the ground
under the pines and dig the hole
for marbles, heel in the soft brown dirt.
You spun like a skater, arms crossed
and absolutely golden hair
tracing the soul's halo around you
then falling to your shoulders.

*   *

No other boys or girls would play with us
when we were together
so you taught me Chinese jump rope
with a chair for a third person.
Then we could always face each other,
dirty knees, a matching missing front tooth each.

*   *

After we drank our coffeemilk
I pulled long vines of pipsissewa
from the soft cushion of needles
in the playground's pine grove
and pretended to tie us together.

*   *

Really we wound ourselves together
as if a living Maypole
and the horse girls came and circled us
at a gallop and laughed at us
thinking what we had done to us
was done by others.

Swimming with Seiger

As a girl she body surfed on the tidal sandbars,
the crest of wave and foam bearing down on her,
the fluid twist, lunge, and launch, the rush
of being borne away, salt water calling back and forth
through her skin.

After years in New England, she moved back
to Wrightsville, but the beach is a different place
to be now, her lost breast harder to hide.
A navy blue one-piece replaces her floral bikini
covering the zipper stitches of surgery.

She rented a beach cottage to hear the waves at night,
a gentle pull toward the water like a calling.
I coaxed her back into the ocean with strong marijuana
the day the reprieve of her remission was revoked.
She was tentative at the edge, back and forth,

until the longing overwhelmed her.
The waves spread and respread themselves
on the shore in inches of foamy smoothness,
came toward us in perfect curls
unrolling glassy green and blue.

Holding hands we went to meet them,
diving under the curls,
waiting for the perfect one to break and carry us.
And it came, gathered us, sucked us up,

turned us over and shot us out toward the shore,
arms out ahead in a hurtling horizontal dive

and then gone,
momentum slowing,
water quieting,
bodies smoothed.

"fighting the lawlessness
that is the necessary companion to

the perfect freedom of strangers"

-Lewis Hyde

Reappearing Act

Pajama feet worn from wandering, my father cut them off.
Took my pajamas so I would not wander, gave them footless
to my brother never realizing it lent him my stealth.

My father broke the bulb in my night light.
Took it, broke the filament, put it back.
I stole my brother's light, my brother stole it back.
Kneeling like praying at the outlet, a useless click and nothing.

My father gave me water from a bottle
poured in my cupped hands.
I never thought to get my own,
wandering free during daylight.
I rationed this night water because I forgot.

My father never woke me, he let the cold do it.
Pulled off the covers from the end of the bed
in a long sweep, a magician's cape in a vanishing act,
watched as I curled in a ball, became invisible.

North, When I Lay Down

He decided to have the world tattooed onto his body,
front and back, breast to knee.
Carolivia, his tattooist, spent ninety-six hours
on the royal blue waters and untouching continents.

Naked before Carolivia he cried like a child
as she performed the cruel art that made him
a masterpiece.

In his clothes, on the street, he knew the hidden world
and envisioned others as solitary planets
in rotation around him.

Newfields, New Hampshire

The signs appeared the evening before,
stretching down Main, every other phone pole,
interspersing themselves with *Lost Dog*
Yard Sale and *Bean Supper*
on ragged cardboard & paper plates,
in royal blue magic marker: *Tattoos.*
They lead to a cottage at the edge of town
where tiger lilies bloom wild orange
and wave on stormy afternoons.

Come 'round back, it says on the sign.
We're open & up late too.

On the back porch
in late afternoon, I think about a tattoo,
small red heart with no initials.
A deer fly bangs its head on the screen,
in a long stumbling buzz.
Wind blows west, smell of eelgrass
and saltwater marsh,
wind blows east, cool pine and cricket flutter,
leaves surge and sway, lilies wave.

Four fat drops fall on the tin porch roof
before the day goes completely liquid.
Heart half done, I rise and walk out
into the rain, swearing I'll return
for the other half.

Unseen Toreador

Black bull
charging every red leaf
falling from a sugar maple

An Uneventful Night in Group

They tell me to work on my anger.
I backhand a small defenseless child.
She has on bell earrings that ring incessantly.
My therapist leaps to her rescue, telling me
I must deal with my "issues" more constructively
or I will jeopardize the "safety" of the group.
I pull out a small pistol and shoot her.
It's only a flesh wound and she will go home
to loved ones, in brave bandages.
The whiner in group
will self-destruct in five seconds.
She's out to get herself and with a little validation
she could be a winner. *You're doing good,* I say.
Then there's Mr. Insight. I poke both his eyes out.
Fuck him for always seeing things so clearly.
And finally there's you.
I'm going to let you live,
because I don't recognize you.

Boys in Blue

If only I still had you,
handsome in your blue suit,
buttons and whistle glinting
like the sparkling tooth of a movie bandito.

If only I still had you,
shot by an estranged husband, between the cold legs
of the wife you'd made warm again.
The precinct boys joked you'd died in the line of duty.

If only I still had you, Daddy
I wouldn't be so obsessed with boys in blue,
their hard and eager bodies, the fullness of their power.
Laughing as they play God over me for a time.

If only I still had you
I wouldn't be longing to lay with them
in the backseats of their cruisers
making empty, angry, obedient love

while the radio barks out its crackling commands
in numeric jargon, my hand holds tightly
to the cage that always separated you
from common criminals.

Compliment

I wanted a clear-breathing day for myself
but we went to the compound instead
to see his parent's collection of wild animals.

It was the tiger I couldn't come away from
as he wandered ahead to the colored birds.
I lingered over the exquisite whiskers,

the jet nose and perfect oval eyes, half-lidded
and soothing to me, so soothing I reached out
to touch the orange smolder of him.

For one moment I identified with his power,
glimpsed this beautiful anger being caged, saw
something of myself;

my boyfriend wound me around himself,
a sensuous accessory in a cage of my own,
a silk scarf of a somebody.

The tiger cocked his head ever so slightly
and bit off the tips of two of my fingers.
Not my hand mind you, just the end

of the pointer, the middle finger's first knuckle,
an afternoon snack in the shade
of a palm, never rising or even chewing.

My boyfriend wanted to shoot the tiger

like you shoot a deer-running dog
or one that bites the baby, but I insisted *No, no,*

random acts never balance out. We'd entered
into something more fated than fingers.

wind•bound / `wind•baund / *adj. Naut.* unable to sail because of contrary winds

Windbound

A sea of slate gray catbirds
in the rattling cattails
bounce in slow motion
perches unfurling
in brown smoke of seed
gone cream

Unrequited Love Letters to My Angel, Alice

1. De rigueur derring-do

My angel,

If ever we are to flee this nomad's no-man's land, these houses upon the hill, it will certainly be together. The lark tells me so in his or her musings aloud. Please say you will be my *untamable cupcake*. Say your passion is equidistant from mine, I mean equal to, and make out, I mean off, with me at your nearest convenience store.

The time is nigh ripe and knee high, white horses extra at some locations. Taxi, tip and destination charges may be slightly higher in your arena. As certain as I am of your swimmability, might I suggest a European moon, honey?

I'm afraid, this is sincere, so meet me, You, tonight at false dawn. I will chirp like a cricket so you'll know it's me. You hoot once like a hoot owl, twice like a screech owl, and I will bring the car 'round.

Travel light, watch your ear, say yes.

2. Dénouement

My angel,

Waiting for you in the bulrushes I got terrible cold and sad.
The meet of the mistry remains on the hoof. The roof tops
beaconed and beckoned, I reckon, and I left without you. Sorry.
At the risk of forwarnedness, I need a backwards cartwheel
as a show of your devotion, a somersault for *maybe devoted*, or just
stand there and look mad if none of this seems to be working for
you. At least bring crackers as a parting gift shot. I roll forward
to meet you with open freesia, wide I'd as the day is twos.
Your wish is at my hand.
I beseech, don't trip or bite. Play fair. Eat cardamom coffee
cake, warm, with butter, and say hi to your basset hound, Angelo,
for me. Look for me by the almond tree. I want poems
by the mistress of purple roses on my birthday.
Until then, then. . . .

A. Tab Rasa

Let a Smile Be Your Undoing

I'm sorry.
That Oreo cookie crumb on your red lip
was an Opening as large as Broadway.
To kiss you so immediately was a vacation
from the timidity I wear.
I know you don't care what my name is
but I guarantee, you will eventually.
Your shadow followed me home,
a child at the supermarket
following the wrong mother.

The Nature of Kisses

When friends kiss
there is no promise
inherent there.

Nothing quickens.
There is no call
to the primordial.

When lovers kiss
part of a soul
is born whispering.

Neurotransmitters,
little geniuses,
are struck dumb.

simply delivered,

baby, a ready riot of sensual fury, any hot number of things
with the truth & your dynamisms that defy. That's you!
Worldly to a faulty perfection you stand alone with everyone
in this fucking city. Stand, simply delivered. An angel baptized
in jazz & pot smoke & the sound of your own bubbles bursting.
Nitroglycerin in your coffee like heavy cream makes you
invincible, explosive. Sweet laughter rolls from your lemon
eyes & fire shines & you catch me like a newspaper page
in a stiff breeze.

en • cyclo • pedia

Anna says, *You have to watch someone*
a long time to know what their toes are doing.
But I don't agree.

You wore black china flats when I met you,
the fronts worn away over your toes.
I fell in love with your feet immediately
and never referred to your face as much.

Your face was full of tricks, but your toes
were an encyclopedia of you.

Their sleepiness and slow morning wander.
In evening, their fresh-scrubbed selves, ready
for clean sheets, their curl in love, their arch in dance,
their dusty sparkle of mica after a day at the beach.

The second time we met, I was juggling.
You were eating ice cream barefoot.
The arc of my sky-blue ball knocked vanilla
from your cone, onto your foot.

I picked up your ice cream. I dropped it back in the cone,
patting it on the head like a small child.

Good as new, you said, taking my wrist,
guiding first my thumb and then my forefinger
to your mouth.

The Miss Florence

Booth 1.   Eating chocolate cake, he smiles
across the table admiring
her chromed choke chain.
Her angry posture causes
its authoritative rattle.
When she brushes her teeth
it sounds like a dog scratching.

Booth 2.   Little boy, five, upturned nose
sprinkled with freckles,
blue eyes cold, watery, vacant.
The barrel of a black plastic
squirt gun in his mouth,
he pumps the trigger furiously
and stares out the window.

Booth 3.   Her red lipstick on the water glass
sends trickles of condensation
down its scratched hourglass
leaving circles of geometric beauty
after many nervous sips.
They hold hands under the table
for a scratched up version
of "In the Mood."

Booth 4.   Roast pork sandwiches
on poppy-seed hard rolls
washed down with Darjeeling
sweetened with brown sugar,
unstirred, dappled with cream.
Downhill, we walk home
swinging held hands.

The Brassiere Salesman's Day Off

Traveling the countryside with a suitcase full of underthings
the brassiere salesman looks forward to his day off. Away

from the crinkle of eager fingers tearing cellophane
releasing the smell of fresh cotton, starch and sizing,

away from the girdles that tuck the tummy and thigh
shaping exquisite womanhood into what it is not,

away from the cross-your-heart models that lift and separate
mixed up with the Victorian models that reign you in.

Breasts and bottoms mean only work to him,
and pulchritude is only so much packaging.

On his day off his wife and he go up by the falls,
picnic on the blanket and catch small trout.

He undresses her at night with sure clean hands
and he never fumbles with her buttons or clasps.

Act One

Today at Macy's, the brunette in the purple velvet dress
looks to have stepped from a rehearsal of *Amadeus*,
her carriage smooth and swirly as a opening curtain.
She moves across the floor, almost choreographed,
her dress an invitation.

On the Daniels Academy stage in sixth grade I was lost
to the play's cast. I played a three line role, my entrance,
the final scene where the hero is resurrected. Sets all to right.
Furnishes the happily-ever-afters. Lines well memorized,
I rolled myself in velvet curtain, reinventing myself over
and over into anyone I ever imagined being.

Now flirting, this velvet brunette flows past me to the escalator,
slowly rises. Turns, all pearls and lipstick, to smile down upon me.
To her I bow deeply. In the velvet of her I am someone else,
a man who knows both sword and piano. A man who throws
a cape over his shoulders and follows into the night. . . .

Cloth

a careful hand,
touching, caressing, gently and everywhere

unabashed grey cashmere
enchanting your nipples

finest fearless silk
imparting tickling kisses
to the backs of your knees

cool cotton on the warm
of your belly as you sleep

the zippered corduroy jumper that nibbles
the top of your spine and back of your neck

Doors Thrown Open to Daisies

Warm slipperiness of us in the car's backseat
hot July afternoon coming home and we cannot wait
for bed's winding sheet and mirror's last glance before we fall.
Instead we have each other smelling of coconut lotion,
spangled with sand and salt crystals, wild wind-styled hair,
bathing suits damp, still cooling our bodies.

White cotton shirt ties arms entangled in hurry,
the light and dark of us tanned and not,
worn like smooth and seamless suits, marks that never leave
our skin, necks salty and offered, the back of this field
haven enough for this whirl of us in a moment of surrender
we practice like children with a white flag.

A Candle Inside

Shivaree

Deep in the leaves minding my own business
& along comes this young farm girl.
Her eyes are blue as cornflowers, like cutouts
& the sky comes through the back of her head.
Her knife shines in the sun & I am picked,
pronounced cute & perfect & off I go.
My insides feel funny. She's pulling them out.
Her knife is sharp, but her hands are warm.
She cuts me some eyes that I'd been missing.
I see the orchard out back, apples bowing the branches.
I see how happy I make her. She fairly glows.
She cuts me a nose & I smell fall leaves,
the rose in her perfume & corn ripening.
She cuts me some ears. I hear a brook
running over its stones, a horse in the pasture
browsing cricketsong in the grass.
Lastly, she cuts me an ear-to-ear grin
and I find I'm pretty pleased I ain't no pie.
With a candle inside I'm nice & warm.
There's a seed left in me starting to itch.

Petroleuse

I have elephantine memories of you
with your Einstein hairdo
and your Thumbelina smile.
The way we ate our M&Ms,
picking out the reds,
yellows and greens,
making rows of stoplights
I ate like a driver hurrying home.
Billiards describes the way I felt
about you and your Molotov
cocktails at happy hour.
You won me with that flash
of tongue, your explosive speech.
The geometry of our collision
was an all-night gas station
into which I pulled my car,
not pushed it.

Cookie

A teenage girl in a red car pulls up her shirt
and shows me her small breast
through the car window.
Just one.
She doesn't look at me though.
This is *supposed* to be unbearably sexy, I think,
this flash.

Like the waitress who showed me
the cloven crotch of her white cotton underpants
during an awkward Chinese split she did
to pick up the butter she dropped,
her eyes looking
directly into mine, smiling, her hand missing
the butter, missing and missing it
while I looked from her eyes to her pussy
to her hand to her eyes.
And she wasn't even waiting on me.

The girl in the red car signals right,
drops back in traffic and exits at Fleur-de-lis.
Without seeing her eyes
this seems a very incomplete interaction.
Her nipple looked forlorn,
like the last small cookie left on a plate.

When Trying

When the radio starts playing my screams I try to turn it
down low, low so it becomes a hum, an undertow, a home.
When the car starts driving me home I try to turn off,
try to signal at the junction, try to break the rearview and
forget where I've been. When a sugar pumpkin asks me
for kisses, I put on orange lipstick, I smile at the candleflame.
I hear the green of the seeds calling. When my shadow starts
walking backwards, tries to get behind me and smile at
trouble, I try to keep an eye on 'em, try to walk with my
back to the sun. When a crow tries to put his shadow on me,
I try to let my wings show, try to walk four-toed, try to sing
a lullabye as best as I can.

It Turned on a Dime Like a Rideable Compass

I will not speak of the tricycle, only say it rolled riderless
down a grassy slope, invisible feet at its pedals.

Sparkled plastic streamers spilling from the black grips
rippling like ponytails in the wind, clapping like a small audience.

A dandelion-fluffed haze was raised in the humming spokes,
the only possible brakes: a tangle of earthly feet.

Notes

pip·sis·se·wa *n.* Algonquin Indian word for prince's or princess pine, once used as a medicinal

shiv·a·ree *n.* 1. a serenade of banging saucepans to newly married persons 2. a medley of sounds, a hubbub

A *petroleuse* was a woman in the French Revolution who demurely firebombed buildings, like Dinesen's Babette.

". . . fighting the lawlessness that is the necessary companion to the perfect freedom of strangers" is a line from *The Gift: Imagination and the Erotic Life of Property* by Lewis Hyde.

"Let A Smile Be Your Undoing" was inspired by Natalie Goldberg and her Oreos in *Writing Down the Bones.*

"Cloth" was inspired by a poem and reading by Jane Shore.

Thanks

My sincerest thanks to Mark Doty, Marie Howe, Kate Johnson, Thomas Lux, Mekeel McBride, Heather McHugh, and Charles Simic for their tutelage, patience, and love of poetry. Thanks to Gordon Carlisle for his art and artfulness. Thanks to Hildy Crill for proofreading. Thanks to Laura Amy Adams, Tom Allen, Susan Carlson, and Susan Poulin. Thanks to all Agrans. Thanks to WUNH 91.3 FM in Durham NH, home of *Bon Mot*, for believing in the power of words.

Dedications

"Responsibility" is for Cinthia G., grammarian extraordinaire.

"Cathedral, Washington DC 1993" is for Frank and Jeff.

"One Circle" is for Peter and Jack.

"Assateague" is for Bill and Stanton, Brooke and family.

"Newly Lost, Newly Found" is for Sarah Ann Wood, Tammy Belanger, and their families.

"Swimming with Seiger" is for Dana, Dave, Jillian, and Leeanne.

"Tethered" is for Kristin and the horse girls.

"An Uneventful Night in Group" is for Cathy, ACSW and pal.

"Compliment" is for Stephanie and the tiger.

"Windbound" is for all my cousins, Brand and Biere.

"Unrequited Love Letters to My Angel, Alice" are for Alice A. and are written by invitation; the phrase *untamable cupcake* is borrowed from James Tate.

"simply delivered" is rather complexly delivered to Amy.

"en • cyclo • pedia" is for all lovely and artful pedestrians, Liza in particular.

About the Author
Rick Agran lives in an apple orchard in Lee, NH with a Jersey steer named Cocoa. He has a whole tricycle as a front door knocker, bakes a mean apple pie, and drinks plenty of cider. He teaches English and Poetry at the University of New Hampshire, New England College, and the Heartwood School of Art. He's the host and producer of Bon Mot, a poetry and spoken word radio program on WUNH-Durham.

About the Book
Crow Milk was typeset in Meridien and Novarese by its author and Tom Allen of Pear Graphic Design, Berwick, Maine. Gordon Carlisle of Carlisle Decorative Arts in Portsmouth, New Hampshire provided the cover illustrations and interior details. Twenty six copies are lettered A-Z and signed by the author and the illustrator.

About the Oyster River Press

Oyster River Press publications are a cooperative undertaking. Authors, editors, illustrators, designers, and translators work together to produce, promote, and premiere a variety of promising manuscripts. Works vary in style and content from traditional to experimental. Drawings, Chinese brushwork, and photography frequently complement the texts. Editorial activities are listed in Literary Market Place and include interviewing and translating services. Books can be ordered directly from the publisher or Koen Book Distributors.

Selections from Oyster River Press

Crow Milk Poems by Rick Agran

Edged In Light Poems by Jane B. Jordan

Halcyon Times Poems on the Birds by Hugh Hennedy

Is It Poison Ivy? by Author/Illustrator Joan R. Darlington

Intense Experience: Social Psychology Through Poetry by Fred Samuels

The Mending of the Sky & Other Chinese Myths Translations by Xiao Ming Li; Illustrated by Shan Ming Wu

Paul Eluard: Ombres et Soleil—Shadows and Sun: Poems and Prose of 1913-1952 Translations by Cicely Buckley, ed., and Lloyd Alexander; Illustrations by Picasso, Magritte, Chagall, and A. Lhote

Peace In Exile Poems by David Oates

Thoughts for the Free Life: Lao Tsu to the Present: Third Edition Edited and illustrated by Cicely Buckley, some original languages with English translations

Selections from Hobblebush Books
distributed by Oyster River Press

What Will We Give Each Other Poems by Sidney Hall, Jr.

Small Town Tales: A Brookline Boyhood Essays by Sidney Hall, Jr.